16-inch model

MACBOOK PRO USER'S GUIDE

FOR BEGINNERS AND SENIORS

UPDATED USER MANUAL WITH TIPS & TRICKS TO GET THE MOST OUT OF YOUR MACBOOK PRO AND macOS CATALINA

SCOTT DOWNING

Goodwater Publishing
279 Stoney Lane
Dallas, TX 75212
Texas
USA

CONTENTS

INTRODUCTION

Apple's 16-inch MacBook Pro laptop debuted on November 2019 as a replacement to the 15-inch MacBook Pro which Apple recalled due to overheating battery issues and a pose to fire safety risk.

The new 16-inch MacBook Pro features a larger 16-inch Retina display, slimmer bezels, an updated keyboard with a scissor mechanism instead of a butterfly mechanism, up to 64GB RAM, up to 8TB of storage, and AMD Radeon Pro 5000M Series graphics cards. It also features a 3072x1920 resolution and a higher pixel density of 226 ppi. The laptop uses Intel's 6 or 8-core 9th-generation processors which is the fastest Apple's MacBook Pro to date.

The Touch Bar and the Retina display of all MacBook Pro models, feature support for True Tone functionality that adjusts white balance to match ambient lighting, and other display features such as wide color support are included.

The new 16-inch MacBook Pro uses the most advanced thermal architecture ever in a Mac notebook models, allowing it to run at higher power for longer periods of time. There's a new fan design with a larger impeller, extended blades, and bigger vents, which increases airflow by 28 percent. The heat sink is also 35 percent larger, allowing for more heat dissipation. All in all, this lets the MacBook Pro sustain up to 12 watts more during intensive workloads compared to the prior 15-inch MacBook Pro.

Design

The 16-inch MacBook Pro features a design that's similar to the earlier MacBook Pro models, but with a slightly larger body and slimmer bezels. It features the same general design elements with large trackpad, thin hinge, Touch Bar, rear Apple logo, side speakers, and silver and space gray color options.

The size and weight of the 16-inch MacBook Pro are 357.90mm x 245.90mm x 16.20mm and 1950.45 grams respectively.

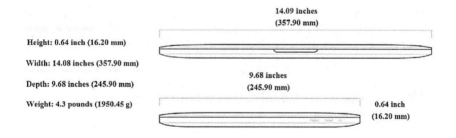

Height: 0.64 inch (16.20 mm)
Width: 14.08 inches (357.90 mm)
Depth: 9.68 inches (245.90 mm)
Weight: 4.3 pounds (1950.45 g)

14.09 inches (357.90 mm)
9.68 inches (245.90 mm)
0.64 inch (16.20 mm)

There's also a new six-speaker sound system in the 16-inch MacBook Pro that's designed to offer the most advanced audio experience ever in a notebook. Sounds are clearer and more natural than ever before, and the bass is half an octave

7

deeper. There's also an upgraded high-performance microphone with a 40 percent reduction in hiss and a better signal to noise ratio.

Displays

The 16-inch MacBook Pro model is designed with a display of about 500 nits brightness, P3 Wide Color support, and True Tone functionality. The True Tone uses a multi-channel ambient light sensor which is able to determine both the brightness of the room and the color temperature. After detecting the white balance, the MacBook Pro is able to adjust both the color and intensity of the display to match the room's lighting for a more natural, paper-like viewing experience that also cuts down on eyestrain.

It features a 3072 x 1920 native resolution at 226 pixels per inch (an improvement compared to the 15-inch MacBook Pro). It also features a variable refresh rate that can be set to the frame rate of a video that's being edited or viewed. Options include 47.95, 48, 50, 59.94, and 60Hz.

Keyboard

The 16-inch MacBook Pro has a redesigned "Magic Keyboard" that does away with the butterfly mechanism that

Apple has been using since 2015. It features a new scissor mechanism which offers 1mm of key travel and a stable key feel, plus an Apple-crafted rubber dome that's designed to store more potential energy for a more responsive key press. The keyboard is similar to the prior keyboards except that there's a physical Escape key instead of a virtual key on the Touch Bar, and the Touch ID button is a separate button too.

The arrow keys have been redesigned as well with an inverted **T** arrangement for the arrow keys, which is a departure from the previous design of the MacBook Pro keyboard. The Touch Bar is also slightly further away from the keys on the keyboard.

Trackpad

As with prior MacBook Pro models, the 16-inch MacBook Pro features a large Force Touch trackpad that takes up much of the bottom of the machines. The Force Touch trackpad has no traditional buttons and is instead powered by a set of Force Sensors, allowing users to press anywhere on the trackpad to get the same response. A Taptic Engine powered by magnets provides users with tactile feedback when using the trackpad, replacing the feel of a physical button press. The Force Touch trackpad supports a light press, which is used as a regular click, along with a deeper press or "force click" as a separate gesture that does things like offer up definitions for a highlighted word.

Touch Bar

There's a Touch Bar on the 16-inch MacBook Pro model. This Touch Bar is a small OLED Retina multi-touch display built into the keyboard and it replaces the row of function keys. It is contextual; meaning what appears on the panel will change, depending on what app you are currently using. It is also customizable, which will allow you to set up different apps.

It also supports True Tone, allowing the white balance to be adjusted to match the ambient lighting conditions. Interacting with the Touch Bar is done through taps, swipes, and other multi-touch gestures, with support for up to 10 fingers at a time available.

Thunderbolt 3 (USB-C) ports

The 16-inch MacBook Pro features four identical Thunderbolt 3 ports. This port is used to charge your MacBook Pro laptop, connect to a display or projector (DisplayPort), and transfer data at Thunder Speed (up to 40 GB/s) or USB transfer (speeds of up to 10 GB/s). Over Thunderbolt 3, the 16-inch MacBook Pro can power two 6K displays at one time or four 4K displays.

Hardware

The 16-inch MacBook Pro is designed with up to an 8-core processor, discrete AMD Radeon Pro 5000M series graphics, up to 64GB RAM, up to 8TB of SSD storage, and a larger, 16-inch display.

- PROCESSOR
  The 16-inch MacBook Pro models are equipped with Intel's 9th-generation 14-nanometer Coffee Lake Refresh chips. The entry-level 16-inch MacBook Pro uses Intel's 6-core 2.6GHz Core i7 processor with Turbo Boost up to 4.5GHz. The higher-end 16-inch MacBook Pro features Intel's 2.3GHz 8-core 9th-generation Core i9 processor with 4.8GHz Turbo

Boost. Both machines can be upgraded to a 2.4GHz 8-core 9th-generation Core i9 processor with Turbo Boost up to 5GHz. According to Apple, its 8-core chips offer up 2.1 times faster performance than a quad-core MacBook Pro and 40 percent more performance than a 6-core MacBook Pro, making them the fastest chips in a Mac notebook ever.

- GPU
  The 16-inch MacBook Pro models feature Intel's built-in UHD Graphics 630, but are also equipped with AMD Radeon Pro 5000M series graphics cards, which are the first 7-nanometer mobile discrete GPUs. The base-level 16-inch MacBook Pro features an AMD Radeon Pro 5300M with 4GB GDDR6 memory and the mid-level model uses an AMD Radeon Pro 5500M with 4GB GDDR6 memory. Both can be upgraded with an AMD Radeon Pro 5500M GPU with 8GB GDDR6 memory.

- RAM
  The 16-inch MacBook Pro supports up to 64GB of 2666MHz DDR4 RAM, which is faster than the RAM used in prior models.

- T2 Chip

T2 chip is included in the 16-inch MacBook Pro model to make them even more secure and to add additional functionality. The T2 chip houses the Secure Enclave processor that protects Touch ID fingerprint data and allows for secure boot and encrypted storage capabilities. It also consolidates multiple controllers, including the system management controller, image signal processor, audio controller, and SSD controller. The T2 chip also powers "Hey Siri" functionality in the 16-inch MacBook Pro. With Hey Siri capabilities, you can say "Hey Siri" to activate the personal assistant on the MacBook Pro without the need to press the physical Siri button.

Battery

Apple's 16-inch MacBook Pro offers "all-day" battery life with up to 11 hours of wireless web usage, up to 11 hours of Apple TV app movie playback, and up to 30 days of standby time. The machine is equipped with a 99.8 watt-hour lithium-polymer battery that's higher capacity than the battery in the recalled 15-inch MacBook Pro model. Apple added extra battery capacity by slightly increasing the thickness of the batteries in the MacBook Pro. The machine comes with a 96W USB-C Power Adapter for charging purposes.

GETTING STARTED

UNBOXING YOUR 16-INCH MACBOOK PRO

What are the accessories that come with the 16-inch MacBook Pro? Make sure to look inside its box and take everything out. This is what is expected to be inside every MacBook Pro box:

1. 96W USB-C Power adapter: The charger adapter that you plug into the wall.
2. USB-C Charge Cable (2 m): Used to extend the reach of the power adapter by attaching it to the power adapter.

COMPUTER LAYOUT

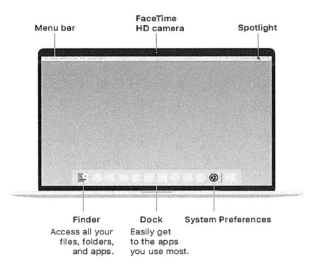

Menu bar

FaceTime
HD camera

Spotlight

Finder
Access all your
files, folders,
and apps.

Dock
Easily get
to the apps
you use most.

System Preferences

Screen

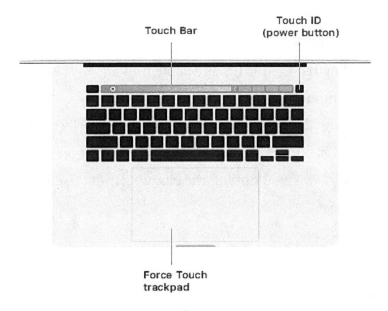

Touch Bar

Touch ID
(power button)

Force Touch
trackpad

Keyboard

CHARGING THE BATTERY

It's very important that you charge the battery before using it for the first time or when it has been unused for extended periods. Always use only the USB-C Charge Cable and 96W USB-C Power Adapter specifically designed for your MacBook Pro laptop. You can also charge your MacBook Pro using any of the Thunderbolt 3 ports on your computer. The battery charges more quickly when the computer is off or in sleep. Incompatible battery, charger, and cable can cause serious injuries or damage to your device. Follow the steps below to charge your MacBook Pro laptop.

1. Connect the USB-C Charge cable to the 96W USB-C Power Adapter.
2. Plug the USB-C Charge cable into any of the computer's Thunderbolt 3 port.
3. Plug the USB-C Power Adapter into an electric socket.
4. After fully charging, disconnect the charger from the device. Then, unplug the charger from the electric socket.

TURNING THE MACBOOK PRO ON AND OFF

Turning the MacBook Pro on

Press and hold the Power button for some seconds to turn on the machine. It takes the MacBook Pro a few moments to start up. When you turn on your machine for the first time, follow the on-screen instructions to set up your laptop.

Turning the MacBook Pro to Sleep or Shutting it Down

When you finish working with your MacBook Pro, you can put it to sleep or shut it down.

Turning the MacBook Pro to Sleep

If you'll be away from your MacBook Pro for only a short time, put it to sleep. When the laptop is in sleep, you can quickly wake it and bypass the startup process. To put your MacBook Pro to sleep, do one of the following:

- Close the display.
- Go to **Apple** menu and click **Sleep** from the **Menu** bar.
- Press the **Power button** and click **Sleep** in the dialog that appears.

Wait a few seconds until the sleep indicator light starts pulsing (indicating that the computer is in sleep and the hard disk has stopped spinning) before moving your MacBook Pro. Moving your computer while the disk is spinning can damage the hard disk, causing loss of data or the inability to start up from the hard disk.

To wake your MacBook Pro:

- If the display is closed, simply open it to wake your MacBook Pro.
- If the display is already open, press the **Power button** or any key on the keyboard.

When your MacBook Pro wakes from sleep, your applications, documents, and computer settings are exactly as you left them.

Shutting Down Your MacBook Pro

If you aren't going to use your MacBook Pro for a couple of days or longer, it's best to shut it down. The sleep indicator light goes on briefly during the shutdown process. To shut down your MacBook Pro, do one of the following:

- Go to **Apple** menu and click **Shut Down** from the **Menu** bar.

- Press the **Power button** and click **Shut Down** in the dialog that appears.

INITIAL SETTING UP OF MACBOOK PRO

When you turn on your machine for the first time, follow the on-screen instructions from the Set up Assistant to set up your new MacBook Pro laptop.

1. Press and hold the Power button for some seconds to turn on the laptop. It takes the MacBook Pro a few moments to start up. After it starts up, **Setup Assistant** opens automatically.
   Setup Assistant helps you enter your Internet and email information and set up a user account on your laptop. If you already have a Mac, Setup Assistant can help you automatically transfer files or folders, applications, and other information from your previous Mac to your new MacBook Pro.
2. Follow the on-screen instructions from the **Set up Assistant** to complete the setup and the desktop will appear.

SET UP AND MANAGE YOUR APPLE ID ACCOUNT

Your Apple ID is the account you use for everything you do

with Apple—including using the App Store, the iTunes Store, iCloud, Messages, and more. Your Apple ID consists of an email address and a password. You need only one Apple ID to use any Apple service, on any device—whether it's your computer, iOS device, iPadOS device, or Apple Watch. It's best to have your own Apple ID and not share it. If you do not have an Apple ID account, you should create one. You can create an Apple ID account using your email address by following the steps below.

1. Go to **Apple** menu   and click **System Preferences** from the Menu bar.
2. Click **Sign In**.
3. Click **Create Apple ID** and follow the on-screen instructions to complete creating your account.

Signing in to your Apple ID Account for an app or website

If you already have an Apple ID account, sign in to your Apple ID account.

1. On your MacBook Pro, click **Sign in with Apple**.
2. Enter your Apple account ID and password and tap **Sign in** or use Touch ID.
3. Follow the on-screen instructions to complete signing in to the app using your Apple ID account.

SETTING UP TOUCH ID

Touch ID is the name of Apple's fingerprint identity sensor on MacBook Pro. It's a form of biometric security that's meant to be more convenient than entering a password. You'll be asked to register a fingerprint for Touch ID as part of the MacBook Pro setup process. You can register up to three fingerprints per user account on your MacBook Pro. Those fingerprints are then encrypted and stored offline in the MacBook Pro's Secure Enclave.

Adding your fingerprint to Touch ID

You can add a fingerprint to Touch ID during setup. To set up Touch ID later or to add additional fingerprints, follow these steps:

1. Go to the **Apple** menu and select **System Preferences**.
2. Select the **Touch ID** preference pane.
3. Click on **Add a fingerprint**.
4. Enter your user password and follow the instructions to register your fingerprint by resting your finger on the Touch ID sensor repeatedly until the registration is complete.

Deleting your fingerprint

1. Go to the **Apple** menu and select **System Preferences**.
2. Select the **Touch ID** preference pane.
3. Hover over the fingerprint icon you wish to delete until you see the **X** in the upper left corner, then click on it.
4. Enter your user password.
5. Press **Delete** to confirm.

Changing your Touch ID settings

Once you add your fingerprint to your MacBook Pro, you'll be able to use your fingerprints to authorize any of the following:

- **Unlock your MacBook Pro** (instead of entering your password).
- Use **Apple Pay** on the Mac
- Authorize purchases from the **iTunes and App Store**.
- **Safari AutoFill**.

By default, all the options are checked, but you can manually change this by unchecking the box next to each option.

1. Go to the **Apple** menu and select **System Preferences**.
2. Select the **Touch ID** preference pane.
3. Check or uncheck the options you prefer.

Logging in using Touch ID

When you first boot up your MacBook Pro laptop, you have to use your password when you log in. After that first login, however, you're free to use Touch ID whenever waking your laptop from sleep.

1. Open your closed MacBook Pro (or press the Touch ID button).
2. Rest your finger on the Touch ID sensor.

SETTING UP SIRI

You can use **Siri** on your MacBook Pro for many tasks by talking to it. For example, you can find files, change preferences, send messages, and add items to your calendar using your voice. On your MacBook Pro, Siri is available whenever you say **Hey Siri** and immediately speak your request, provided the MacBook Pro lid is open.

Enabling Siri

Enabling **Siri** is very easy but it is worthy to note that to use Siri, your MacBook Pro must be connected to the internet

1. Clicking **Siri** 🔘 in the menu bar opens Siri, if you enabled it during setup. If you didn't enable it during setup, follow the steps below to enable it.
2. Go to Apple menu and click the **System Preferences** 🔘.
3. Click **Siri**, then select **Enable Ask Siri**.
4. You can set other preferences in the Siri pane, such as:

- **Use Siri when your MacBook Pro is locked**: You can choose to use Siri even if your MacBook Pro is locked or in sleep by selecting **Allow Siri when locked** checkbox.

- **Set a keyboard shortcut**: Click the Keyboard Shortcut pop-up menu, then choose a different shortcut to ask Siri or create your own. By default, the keyboard shortcut to ask Siri is to press and hold the Command key and the Space bar at the same time.

- **Choose how Siri communicates**: Click the Language pop-up menu, then choose a language. Click the Siri Voice pop-up menu, then choose the gender (and sometimes dialect) that Siri speaks.

- **Mute Siri**: Click **Off** next to **Voice Feedback**—the response from Siri is shown in the Siri window but not spoken.
- **Add Siri to the menu bar**: Select the **Show Siri in menu bar** checkbox.

Ask Siri

To ask Siri on your MacBook Pro, you can do any of the following:

- Click **Siri** in the **Menu** bar (or use the Touch Bar) and start speaking.
- Press and hold the **Command** key ⌘ and the **Space bar**, and speak to Siri.
- Say **Hey Siri** and ask your MacBook Pro laptop what you want it to do for you.
  Hey Siri doesn't respond when the lid to your MacBook Pro laptop is closed. If the lid is closed and connected to an external display, you must invoke Siri from the icon in the menu bar.

Ways to use Siri

You can ask Siri questions on your MacBook Pro to quick answers or to do a task for you. Here are some examples:

Say something like	Description
Open Notes	Siri immediately opens the **Notes** app for you.
Show me my passwords	Siri opens the Passwords pane in Safari on your MacBook Pro.
Create a note (and then dictate what you want to write).	Have Siri write a note or email for you.
Create a meeting for today at 2 p.m.	Have Siri set up a meeting for you.
Where's the nearest grocery store?	When Location Services is enabled in Privacy preferences, Siri can give you information based on your current location or include maps to give you more details.
Increase my screen brightness.	Siri can automatically change some preferences or open a preference pane for you.
How fast is my	Siri can give you information

Mac? Or **How much free space do I have?**	about your MacBook Pro.

TRANSFERRING DATA FROM YOUR PREVIOUS COMPUTER

You can seamlessly transfer your files and settings from your old Mac or PC to your new MacBook Pro. You can transfer these information to your MacBook Pro wirelessly or with an Ethernet cable and adapters.

Transferring data wirelessly

You can transfer data from your previous machine to your new MacBook Pro wirelessly using **Set up Assistant**. To do that later, you can use **Migration Assistant** by following these steps:

1. Connect the two computers to the same network and make sure both computers are near each other throughout the migration process.
2. Open a **Finder** window and go to **Applications/Utilities**.
3. Double click **Migration Assistant** and follow the on-screen instructions to complete the wireless migration.

Transfer using Ethernet

You can transfer your data over Ethernet using a USB-C to Ethernet adapter to connect the Ethernet cable to your MacBook Pro.

Connect the other end of the Ethernet cable to your other computer. Before transferring your data using Ethernet, make sure your MacBook Pro battery is fully charged.

Copy files from a USB storage device

Connect the external storage device to your MacBook Pro using a USB-C to USB Adapter and drag the files from your storage device to your MacBook Pro.

Backing up and restoring data using Time Machine

To keep your files safe, it's important to back up your MacBook Pro regularly. The easiest way to back up is to use Time Machine—which is built into your MacBook Pro—with an external storage device connected to your MacBook Pro. Time Machine can also back up your Mac contents to supported network volumes.

To set up Time Machine, follow these steps:

1. Make sure your MacBook Pro is on the same Wi-Fi network as your external storage device, or connect your external storage device to your MacBook Pro.
2. Click the **System Preferences** 🌐 in the Dock, click **Time Machine**.
3. Select **Back Up Automatically** and select the drive you want to use for backup. That's all.

NOTIFICATION CENTER

Notification Center on your MacBook Pro shows two views: Today view and Notifications view. Today view shows details about your day which include appointments, weather, birthdays, even a summary of what you have planned for tomorrow while Notifications view shows notifications you missed.

To use Today view in Notification Center:

1. Click the **Notification Center** ≔ in the Menu bar, or swipe left with two fingers from the right edge of the trackpad.
2. In Notification Center, click **Today**.
3. Click an item in a widget to see its details or take an action.

For example, click an item in the Weather widget to show the hourly and five-day forecasts. Or click a reminder's checkbox to complete it.

4. You can do any of the following to customize the Today view:

- **Customize a widget**: Move the pointer over the widget, then click the **Info button** ⓘ that appears.

- **Reorder widgets**: Click **Edit** at the bottom of Today view, then drag a widget up or down.

- **Add or remove widgets**: Click **Edit** (or the new widget count, if shown) at the bottom of Today view. To add an available widget, click its **Add button** ⊕ . To remove a widget, click its **Remove button** ⊖ ; the widget is moved to the list of available widgets.

- **Get more widgets**: Click **Edit** at the bottom of Today view, click **App Store**, then buy or download widgets.

To use Notifications view in Notification Center:

1. Click the **Notification Center** ≔ in the Menu bar, or swipe left with two fingers from the right edge of the trackpad.

2. In Notification Center, click **Notifications**.

3. Click a notification to open the item in the associated app. For example, click a Mail notification to open the email in Mail. When you open an item, it's removed from Notifications view. To remove an item without opening it, move the pointer over it, then click the **Clear button** ✕ .

DOCK

The Dock on the Mac desktop is a convenient place to access apps and features (like Siri, Launchpad, and the Trash) that you're likely to use every day. The Dock can show up to three recently used apps that aren't already in the Dock and a folder for items you download from the internet.

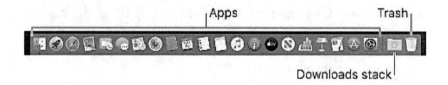

Open items in the Dock

In the Dock on your MacBook Pro, you can do any of the following:

- **Open an app**: Click the app icon. For example, to open the Finder, click the **Finder icon** in the Dock.

- **Open a file in an app**: Drag the file over an app's icon. For example, to open a document you created in Pages, drag the document over the Pages icon in the Dock.

- **Show an item in the Finder**: Command-click the item's icon.

- **Switch to the previous app and hide the current app**: Option-click the current app's icon.

- **Switch to another app and hide all other apps**: Option-Command-click the icon of the app you want to switch to.

You can Control-click an item to display a shortcut menu of other actions to take, such as open or close an app, open a recent document, and more.

If an app stops responding, you can Force Quit the app from the Dock (you may lose unsaved changes). Control-Option-click the app's icon, then choose **Force Quit**.

Add or remove Dock items

On your MacBook Pro laptop, you can do any of the

following:

- **Add an item to the Dock**: Drag apps to the left side of (or above) the line that separates the recently used apps. Drag files and folders to the right side of (or below) the other line that separates recently used apps. An alias for the item is placed in the Dock.

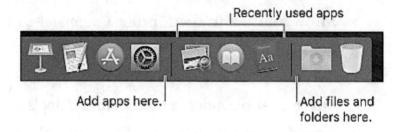

Recently used apps

Add apps here. Add files and folders here.

- **Remove an item from the Dock**: Drag the item out of the Dock until you see Remove. Only the alias is removed; the actual item remains on your Mac. If you accidentally remove an app icon from the Dock, it's easy to put it back (the app is still on your Mac). Open the app to make its icon appear again in the Dock. Control-click the app's icon, then choose **Options** and select **Keep in Dock**.
- You can also rearrange items in the Dock—just drag an item to a new location.

FINDER

The Finder is the home base for your MacBook Pro computer. It helps you to see and organize your files on the MacBook Pro laptop. The Finder icon looks like a blue smiling face; click the icon in the Dock to open a Finder window.

Click to open

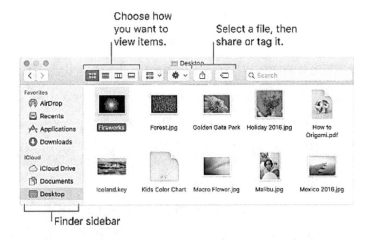

Finder sidebar

Customize the Finder toolbar

Follow the steps below to customize the Finder toolbar

1. Click the **Finder icon** in the Dock to open a Finder window.

2. Do any of the following:

   - **Hide or show the toolbar**: Click **View** and select **Hide Toolbar**, or click **View** and select **Show Toolbar**.

     Hiding the toolbar also hides the sidebar, and moves the status bar from the bottom to the top of the window.

   - **Resize the toolbar**: If you see angle brackets >> at the right end of the toolbar, it means the window is too small to show all of the toolbar items. Enlarge the window or click the brackets to see the rest of the items.

   - **Change what's in the toolbar**: Click **View** and select **Customize Toolbar**. You can drag items into and out of the toolbar, add a space between items, and choose whether to show text with the icons.

   - **Rearrange the items in the toolbar**: Press and hold the Command key, then drag an item to a new location.

   - **Add a file or an app**: Press and hold the Command key, then drag the item to the Finder toolbar until you see a green plus sign.

- **Remove an item**: Press and hold the Command key, then drag the item out of the toolbar.

TOUCH BAR

The Touch Bar on your MacBook Pro computer can use familiar gestures—like tap, swipe, or slide—directly on the Touch Bar to adjust settings, use Siri, access function keys, and do tasks in different apps. It replaces the row of function keys.

Touch Bar basics

The Control Strip, at the right end of the Touch Bar, lets you adjust common settings—like brightness and volume—and ask Siri. You can expand it to access additional settings and features. The other buttons available in the Touch Bar depend on the app you're using or the task you're doing.

- **Change the brightness or volume, or ask Siri**: Tap the buttons in the Control Strip. For brightness and volume, you can also quickly flick left or right on the buttons.

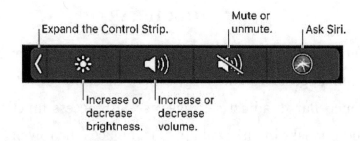

- **Expand the Control Strip**: Tap the **Expand button** < in the Expanded Control Strip to access additional settings and features like Mission Control and Launchpad, or to control video or music playback. For some settings—such as display brightness—you can touch and hold the button to change the setting.

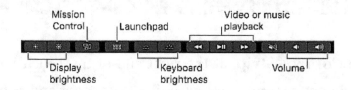

Use other buttons: Tap buttons to quickly do tasks in the app you're using. Each app is different—try it out to see what you can do. For example, here's how the Touch Bar looks when you select a file in the Finder:

And here's how it looks when you view a picture in the Photos app:

ACCESSIBILITY FEATURES

MacBook Pro is designed with accessibility features to help people with disabilities get the most out of their new machine. With built-in support for vision, hearing, mobility, and learning, you can create and do amazing things.

To enable accessibility features on your MacBook Pro, follow these steps.

- Go to **Apple** menu and select **System Preferences**.
- Select **Accessibility** . Then select and turn on the features you want to use.

  Some of the features include:

  Voice Control: This feature helps you to use your voice to make things happen. You can quickly open and interact with apps, search the web, and write and edit more efficiently with rich text editing commands. So you can simply say, **Move up two lines. Select previous word. Capitalize that**. And your MacBook Pro does it.

VoiceOver: This feature is a revolutionary built-in screen reader that's more than a text-to-speech tool. It tells you exactly what's on your screen and talks you through actions like editing a video, building a presentation, or quickly navigating from one app to another.

Hover Text: This feature helps you get a quick size boost of what you're reading.
Hover Text makes it easier to view text on your display. If a paragraph, caption, or headline is too small to read, just hover over it with your cursor and press Command. You'll get a dedicated window with a large, high-resolution version of your selection. You can even choose the fonts and colors that work best for you.

Text to Speech: If you learn better when you can hear what you're reading or writing, this feature lets you highlight any text and have your MacBook Pro read it aloud. And you can choose from more than 70 male or female voices across 42 languages.

APPS

Your MacBook Pro laptop comes with a collection of great apps already installed so you can have fun, work, connect with friends, get organized, buy things, and more. It also comes with apps that can enable you to be creative and productive right from the start. Some of these apps that come with your MacBook Pro are described below.

FACETIME

FaceTime app enables you to make video and audio calls from your MacBook Pro. This app enables you to make video or audio call. Make sure this feature is turned on.

Follow these steps to make FaceTime call.

1. Go to **FaceTime** app and enter your Apple ID and password.
2. Click **Sign in** and the **FaceTime** is on automatically.
3. In the field at the top of the FaceTime window, enter the email address or phone number of the person you want to call. You may need to press **Return**.
4. To start the FaceTime call, click the Video button or the Audio button .

To receive FaceTime calls:

1. Assuming your **FaceTime** app is open and you're signed in, when someone calls you: you will see a pop-up window. If FaceTime is closed, you'll see a notification in the top-right corner.
2. The notification will tell you who's calling if you have their details in the **Contacts** app.
3. If you want to speak with them, click **Accept** and when you want to end the call click the red handset icon

MESSAGES

You can send messages with text, photos, and other files to your friends on MacBook Pro laptop. You will need to set up the laptop to send texts to people before you can use it to send text messages with iMessage. Follow these steps to set it up:

1. Go to **Messages** app on your MacBook Pro laptop and select **Messages**.
2. Click **Preferences** and select **iMessage**.
3. Enter your Apple ID and password, then click **Next**. Make sure the Apple ID is the same Apple ID you're using on your other devices.
4. After signing in, select the following options:

- **Store your messages in iCloud**: Select **Enable Messages in iCloud**.
- **You can be reached for messages at**: Select the email addresses or phone numbers you want people to be able to use to send you texts on your MacBook Pro laptop using iMessage.
- **Send read receipts**: If you select this, people who send you messages will see when you've read them.
- **Start new conversations from**: Choose the email address or phone number that you want to use for starting new conversations.

Sending texts to people: follow these steps to send texts to people.

1. Go to **Messages** app 💬 on your MacBook Pro laptop, click the **Compose button** 📝 to start a new message (or use the Touch Bar).
2. Do one of the following:
   - **Send a message to one person**: Type a name, an email address or a phone number in the **To** field. As you type, Messages suggests matching addresses from your **Contacts** app or from people you've previously sent messages to.

You can also click the **Add button** ⊕ to the right of the **To** field. Click a contact in the list, then click the email address or phone number.

- **Send a message to more than one person**: If you're sending a group message via iMessage, everyone in the group must have a phone number or an email address registered with iMessage.

3. Enter your message in the field at the bottom of the window. You can include any of the following:

- **Text**: Type text in the message field.

- **Photos or videos on your MacBook Pro**: Drag photos (including Live Photos) or videos to the message field, or copy and paste them.
  It is worthy to note that if you drag a Live Photo to your message, friends see only a still photo. If you want friends to be able to see the Live Photo play, share it from the **Photos** app.

- **Files or web links**: Drag or copy and paste files or web links.

- **Emoji**: Click the **Emoji button** ☺ to add emoji to your message. If you add three or fewer emoji, they appear as large emoji.

4. Press **Return** on your keyboard to send the message.

MAIL

Mail app enables you to send, receive, and manage email for all of your email accounts in one location. Simply add the accounts—such as iCloud, Exchange, Google, school, work, or other—you want to use in Mail.

Add an email account

1. The first time you open the **Mail** app  on your MacBook Pro laptop, it may prompt you to add an account. Select an account type—if you don't see your type, select Other Mail Account—then enter your account information.

Choose a Mail account provider...

○ **iCloud**

○ 🄴🅇 Exchange

○ Google⁻

○ YAHOO!

○ **Aol.**

○ Other Mail Account...

(?)   Cancel   Continue

2. If you already added an email account, you can still add more. To add an account, follow these steps.

    • Go to **Mail** app and select **Add Account**.

- Select an account type, then enter your account information. Make sure the Mail checkbox is selected for the account.

Temporarily stop using an email account

- Go to **Mail** app and select **Accounts**.
- Select the account, then deselect the Mail checkbox. Now the account's messages are not shown in Mail. To use the account again with Mail, select the Mail checkbox; the account's messages are shown again (they don't need to be downloaded from the server again).

Remove an email account

When you remove an email account from Mail, the account's messages are deleted and no longer available on your MacBook Pro laptop.

- Go to **Mail** app and click **Preferences**.
- Click **Accounts** and select the account to be removed.
- Click the **Remove button** — .

Write and send emails in Mail on Mac

When you write a message, you can add recipients, text, photos, and more, before sending your message.

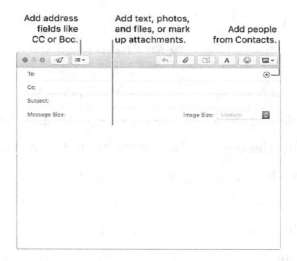

1. Go to **Mail** app and click **New Message button** in the Mail toolbar (or use the Touch Bar).

2. In an address field (such as **To** or **Cc**) of your message, type names or email addresses of the person(s) you want to send it to.

   To use other fields, such as **Bcc** or **Priority**, click the **Header button** ≡ ⌄ , then click a field.

3. Enter the subject of your message, then add your text. You can do any of the following:

   - Click the **Format button** A (or use the Touch Bar) to quickly change fonts and styles.

- Click the **Emoji button** ☺ (or use the Touch Bar) to easily add emoji and symbols.
- Click the **Attachment button** 📎 or the **Photo Browser button** 🖼 ˅ to add photos or documents.

4. When you're ready to send your message, click the **Send button** 📨 (or use the Touch Bar).

SAFARI

Safari app is the fastest and most efficient way to surf the web on your MacBook Pro laptop. An updated start page includes Favorites, frequently and recently visited websites, Siri Suggestions for relevant websites in your browsing history, bookmarks, Reading List, iCloud tabs, and links sent to you in Messages.

Go to websites using Safari

With Safari app, it's easy to get to the websites you want. Follow these steps to go to a webpage.

1. Go to **Safari** app 🧭 and enter the page's name or URL you want to search in the Smart Search field. As you type, Safari Suggestions appear.

Enter a page's name or URL

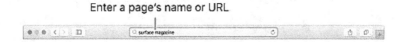

2. Pick a suggestion, or press **Return** to go directly to the address you typed.

Make Safari your default web browser

When you click links in emails and other documents, they open in your default browser. Safari is the default browser when you first set up your MacBook Pro, but another browser you install can become the default unexpectedly. To make Safari your default web browser, follow these steps.

1. Go to **Apple** menu and select **System Preferences**.
2. Click **General**.
3. Click the **Default web browser** pop-up menu and choose **Safari**.

Customize the Safari browser window

You can change the layout of Safari bars, buttons, and bookmarks to suit your browsing style.

1. **Use the Favorites bar**
   - Go to **Safari** app ◍ , choose **View** and select **Show Favorites Bar**.
2. **Show the status bar**
   - Go to **Safari** app ◍ , choose **View** and select **Show Status Bar**.

     When you hold the pointer over a link, the status bar at the bottom of the Safari window shows the link's full address.

PHOTOS

You can use Photos app to organize, edit, and share your photos and videos, and keep your entire photo library up to date on all your devices. With Photos, it's easy to organize albums, find just the photo that you're looking for, and make beautiful slideshows and photo gifts. With Photos app, you can store your photos and videos in your MacBook Pro laptop and in iCloud using iCloud Photos.

Turn on iCloud Photos

If you're not already signed in with your Apple ID, make you sign in. after signing in, click iCloud in the Apple ID preferences sidebar, then select Photos in the list of apps.

Follow these steps to turn iCloud Photos in Photos app.

1. Go to **Photos** app 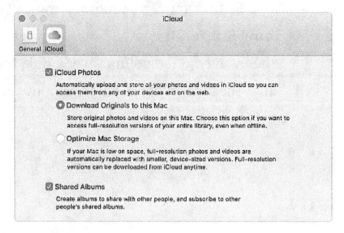 and choose **Photos**.
2. Click **Preferences** and select **iCloud**.
3. Select the iCloud Photos checkbox.

4. Select one of the following options:
   - **Download Originals to this Mac**: this option stores the full-size versions of your photos both on your MacBook Pro and in iCloud.
   - **Optimize Mac Storage**: this option stores smaller versions of your photos on your MacBook Pro when storage space is limited, and keeps the original, full-size photos in iCloud. Choose this option to conserve space on your MacBook Pro. To restore the originals to your laptop, just select **Download Originals to this Mac**.

Browse and view photos in Photos on Mac

Photos uses Days, Months, and Years views to organize your photos and videos by time and location. When displaying photos, Photos automatically hides similar photos and reduces clutter by removing items such as screenshots and receipts so you can focus on your best shots. Click Days to see photos and videos taken on the same day. Click Months to see photos and videos grouped by month and day. Click Years to quickly access photos taken in the same year. You can also view photos individually to see more detail, switch to a full-screen view, and hide the photos you don't want to work with.

To browse Photos by day, month, or year:

1. Go to **Photos** app , click **Photos** in the sidebar, then click **Days**, **Months**, or **Years** in the toolbar.

2. Double-click a day, month, or year to see the photos in it. On a trackpad, you can pinch open or closed on the day, month, or year to change views.

3. Do any of the following:
   - **Scroll up or down in a view**: Press the Up Arrow or Down Arrow key. On a trackpad, swipe up or down with two fingers.
   - **Change the size of thumbnails**: Drag the Zoom slider, or pinch in or out on the trackpad.

- **Play a movie or show a map of the photos**: Click ⊙ and choose **Play Movie** or **Show Map**.

Hide photos from view

You can hide selected photos and show them only when you want to work with them.

1. Go to **Photos** app 🌑 and click **Photos** in the sidebar.
2. Select the photo or photos, choose **Image** and click **Hide [number] Photos**.
3. Click **Hide Photos**. The selected photos disappear from view but are not deleted.

To show hidden photos, choose **View** and select **Show Hidden Photo Album**. The Hidden album appears in the sidebar. To unhide photos in it, select them, then choose **Image** and select **Unhide [number] Photos**.

Edit a photo

You can use the Photos editing tools to easily make simple changes to your photos, such as rotating them or cropping them to get the best framing.

To edit a photo, follow these steps.

1. In the **Photos** app   you can do one of the following:

   - Double-click a photo thumbnail, then click **Edit** in the toolbar.

   - Select a photo thumbnail, then press **Return**.

2. You can also do any of the following:

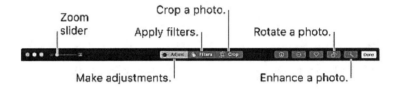

- **Zoom in or out on a photo**: Click or drag the Zoom slider.

- **Make adjustments**: Click **Adjust** to display the adjustment tools.

- **Apply filters**: Click **Filters** to display filters you can apply to change the look of your photo.

- **Crop the image**: Click **Crop** to display the options for cropping a photo.

- **Rotate a photo**: Click the **Rotate button** in the toolbar to rotate the image counterclockwise. Option-click the button to rotate the image clockwise.

- **Automatically enhance a photo**: Click the **Enhance button** to have the color and contrast of your photo adjusted automatically. To remove the changes, press **Command-Z** or **click Revert to Original**.

3. To stop editing, click **Done** or press **Return**.

NOTES

Notes are more than just text. Jot down quick thoughts, or add checklists, images, web links, and more. Shared folders let you share an entire folder of notes with a group, and everyone can participate.

Write a new note

You can write notes and change the formatting in a note—for example, change the font size or alignment, or make text bold.

1. Go to **Notes** app and click **Notes** in the sidebar.
2. Click the folder where you want to put the note and click the **New Note** in the toolbar (or use the Touch Bar).
3. Type your note.
4. When you're done typing, click **Save** button.

Lock a note

You can lock notes you want to keep private on your

MacBook Pro laptop, so only people who know the password can view them. You create a password, and then use it to lock or unlock any note. Follow these steps to set up a password.

1. Go to **Notes** app   and click **Notes** in the sidebar.
2. Click **Preferences** and select **Set Password**.
3. Enter a password in the **Password field**, then enter it again in the **Verify field**.
4. Enter a hint to help you remember the password. The hint appears if you enter the wrong password three consecutive times.
5. Click **Set Password**.

Once you set up a password, you can lock your notes following these steps.

1. Go to **Notes** app   and select the note you want to unlock.
2. Click the **Lock button** 🔒 and select **Lock Note**.
3. Enter the password.

To remove the lock from a note, follow these steps.

1. Select the locked note and click the **Lock button** 🔒 .
2. Select **Remove Lock**, and enter the password.
3. Click the **Remove Lock** button 🔓 to unlock the note.

PODCASTS

You can use Apple Podcasts to browse, download, subscribe, and listen to favorite podcasts on your MacBook Pro laptop. To do any of these, you must first sign in with your Apple ID

Sign in to Podcasts

1. Go to **Podcasts** app and click your **Account**.
2. Click **Sign In**, then enter your Apple ID and password.
   If you already signed in to **Music** or the **Apple TV** app, you're automatically signed in to **Podcasts**.
3. Click **Next**.

Listen to podcasts

Podcasts are free audio shows that you can stream and play on your Mac. You can listen to individual episodes, or you can subscribe to a show so that new episodes are automatically downloaded as they become available. Your podcast subscriptions, stations, and current play position sync to the Podcasts app on all your devices when you sign in with the same Apple ID.

Follow these steps to listen to an episode.

1. Go to **Podcasts** app and click your **Listen Now** in the sidebar.

2. Hold the pointer over the show or episode you want to play, then click the **Play button** ▶ .

When the episode plays, you see the playback controls at the top of the Podcasts window.

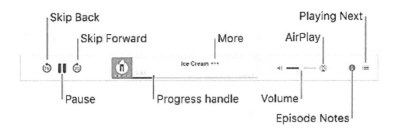

3. Do any of the following with the playback controls:

   • **Skip forward or skip back within the episode**: Drag the **Progress Handle** right (to skip forward) or left (to skip back), or use the Touch Bar.
   You can also use the **Skip Back button** ⟲ to go back (in 15-second increments) and the **Skip Forward button** ⟳ to skip ahead (in 30-second increments) in the episode.

   • **Pause the episode**: Click the **Pause button** ‖ (or use the Touch Bar).
   Click the **Play button** ▶ to resume playback (or use the Touch Bar).

- **Change the audio output**: Click the **AirPlay button** to choose which speakers to use to listen to the podcast.

- **Manage the episode** *example, copy the link, share the episode, or go to the Show page)*: Hold the pointer over the episode playing, click the **More button** , then choose an option.

- **Read the episode description**: Click the **Episode Notes button** .

Subscribe to podcasts

You can subscribe to podcasts you like and get new episodes automatically as soon as they become available. They're free of charge.

To subscribe, follow these steps.

1. Go to **Podcasts** app and search to find podcasts, or click an item under Apple Podcasts in the sidebar on the left.

2. Select a show to see its information page, then click the **Subscribe button** + Subscribe .

To unsubscribe from a podcast, follow this step.

- Click the **More button**   , then choose **Unsubscribe**.

Download podcast episodes

You can download specific episodes so you can play them when you're offline, even if you don't subscribe to the podcast. Follow these steps to download podcast episodes.

1. Go to **Podcasts** app and search to find podcasts, or click an item under Apple Podcasts in the sidebar on the left.
2. Do one of the following:
   - Control-click an episode, then choose **Add To Library**.
   - Hold the pointer over an episode, then click the **Add button** .
     It is important to note that you may need to select a show to see its episodes.
3. To download the episode, click the **More button** then choose **Download Episode**.
   Optionally, you can click the **Download button** next to the item.

To remove a downloaded episode, follow this step.

- Click the **More button**   , then choose **Remove**.

FIND MY

You can use Find My to locate your friends, family, and Apple devices—all in the same app.

Before you can share your location with your friends and find your devices, you need to turn on Location Services and Find My Mac. You can do this when you open Find My for the first time or later in System Preferences.

Follow these steps to turn on Location Services

1. Go to **Apple** menu , choose **System Preferences** and click **Security & Privacy**.
2. Click **Privacy**, then click **Location Services** on the left.
3. Click the **lock icon** to unlock it, then enter an administrator name and password.
4. Select **Enable Location Services**, then select **Find My** in the list of apps.

Set up Find My

Follow these steps to set up Find My

1. Go to **Apple** menu , choose **System Preferences** and click **Apple ID**.

If you don't see Apple ID, click Sign In, then sign in with your Apple ID.

2. Click **iCloud** in the sidebar.

3. Select **Find My**, then click **Allow** (if asked) to allow Find My Mac to use the location of your MacBook Pro.

If a **Details button** is next to Find My Mac, make sure you turned on **Location Services** and **Find My** in **Security & Privacy** preferences.

Turn on Find My options

On your MacBook Pro, follow these steps to turn On Find My options.

1. Go to **Apple** menu , choose **System Preferences** and click **Apple ID**.
   If you don't see Apple ID, click Sign In, then sign in with your Apple ID.

2. Click **iCloud** in the sidebar.

3. Select **Find My**, then click **Options**.
   If you see a **Details button**, you need to set up Find My.

4. Turn any of the following on or off:

- **Find My Mac**: Turning this option on allows you to locate your Mac if you misplace it, and protect the information on it.
- **Offline Finding**: Turning this option on allows you to locate your device (using Bluetooth) even when it isn't connected to Wi-Fi or cellular.
  Note: When you turn off Offline Finding, your Mac can't be found by you or anyone else.

Locate a device in Find My on Mac

In Find My, you can see the location of a missing device, and play a sound on it to help you find it. You must note that to locate a missing device, you must add it in Find My before it's lost.

Follow these steps to see the location of a device.

1. Go to **Find My** app 🔘 and click **Devices**.
2. In the Devices list, select the device you want to locate.
   - **If the device can be located**: It appears on the map so you can see where it is.
   - **If the device can't be located**: Below the device's name, "No location found" appears. If you want to be notified when the location is available, click the **Info button** ⓘ on the map,

then select **Notify When Found**. You receive a notification once it's located.

Get directions to a device

Follow these steps to get directions to the device.

1. Go to **Find My** app and click **Devices**.
2. In the Devices list, select the device you want to get directions to, then click the **info button** on the map.
3. Click **Directions**.

   The **Maps** app opens with the directions from your location to the device's current location.

16-INCH MACBOOK PRO TIPS & TRICKS

How to conserve battery power

To extend battery life on a given charge, you can reduce the display brightness, close apps, and disconnect peripheral devices you're not using. You can change your power settings in Energy Saver preferences (click the **System Preferences** in the Dock, then click **Energy Saver**). If your MacBook Pro is in sleep when a device is connected to it, the device's battery may drain.

How to choose light or dark appearance (How to adjust Dark Mode)

If you want to change the choice you made when you set up your Mac Pro computer, follow these steps to change the set up:

1. Click **System Preferences** in the **Dock**, or click **Apple** menu and select **System Preferences**.
2. Click **General**, and then select **Light**, **Dark**, or **Auto** for your appearance. You can also set other appearance preferences here.

How to change Notification settings

On your MacBook Pro laptop, you can change the Notification settings to specify when you don't want to be disturbed by notifications, and to control how apps show notifications and how they're sorted in Notification Center. Follow these steps to change the settings.

1. Go to **Apple** menu and select **System Preferences**.

2. Click **Notifications** and select any of the options below to view or change the settings.

   - **Do Not Disturb**: Stop notifications during the time range you specify, when the display is sleeping, or when you're projecting the screen. Select checkboxes to receive call notifications even when Do Not Disturb is on.

   - **Allow Notifications from**: Turn an app's notifications on or off. When you turn them off, the app's alert style and other notification options are dimmed.

   - **Alert style**: Select a style for the app's notifications:

     o **None**: Notifications don't appear on the screen.

     o **Banners**: Notifications appear on the screen and disappear after a while.

- o **Alerts**: Notifications stay on the screen until you dismiss them.
- **Show notifications on lock screen**: When you wake your MacBook Pro laptop from sleep, app notifications you received while it was sleeping are shown in the login window.
- **Show notification preview**: Show a preview in the notification. For example, if you receive an email, you see a preview of the email in the Mail notification.

  If you chose to show notifications on the lock screen, you can choose when to show the preview.
  - o **when unlocked**: Previews are shown only when you're logged in to your user account.
  - o **always**: Previews are always shown (even in the login window).

How to use Handoff on your MacBook Pro

Handoff enables you to continue on one device where you left off on another. For example, work on a presentation on your MacBook Pro, then continue on your iPad. Or start an email message on your iPhone, then finish it on your MacBook Pro. View a message on your Apple Watch, and respond to it on your MacBook Pro. You don't have to worry about transferring files. When your MacBook Pro and devices are near each other, an icon appears in the Dock whenever an activity can be handed off; to continue, just click the icon.

Click to continue what you were doing on your iPhone.

Follow these steps to turn on Handoff on your MacBook Pro and other devices but make sure your MacBook Pro, iOS device, or iPadOS device have Wi-Fi and Bluetooth turned on and are signed in with the same Apple ID.

1. **On your MacBook Pro**:
   - Go to **Apple** menu and select **System Preferences**.
   - Click General and select **Allow Handoff between this Mac and your iCloud devices** (below **Recent items**).
   - To turn it off, deselect the option.

2. **On iPad, iPhone, or iPod touch**:
   - Go to **Settings** and select **General**.
   - Tap **Handoff** and tap to turn on Handoff.
   - To turn it off, tap the option.

3. **On Apple Watch**:

- Open the **Watch** app on iPhone and go to My Watch.

- Tap **General** and tap to turn on **Enable Handoff**.

- To turn it off, tap the option.

How to unlock your MacBook Pro and approve requests with Apple Watch

When you're wearing your Apple Watch, you can use it to automatically unlock your MacBook Pro and approve authentication tasks—such as entering passwords, unlocking notes and preferences, and authorizing installations—without having to type a password. These features use strong encryption to provide secure communication between your Apple Watch and MacBook Pro.

To use these features (Auto Unlock and Approve with Apple Watch), make sure

- You're signed in to your MacBook Pro and Apple Watch with the same Apple ID.

- Your Apple Watch is unlocked and running watchOS 3 or later to automatically unlock your MacBook Pro; approving authentication requests requires watchOS 6.

- Two-factor authentication is turned on for your Apple ID.

To turn on two-factor authentication, go to **Apple** menu, select **System Preferences**, click **Apple ID**, choose **Password & Security**, then select **Set Up Two-Factor Authentication**.

Turn on Auto Unlock and Approve with Apple Watch

- Choose **Apple** menu , choose **System Preferences**, and then click **Security & Privacy**.
- Click **General**, then select **Use your Apple Watch to unlock apps and your Mac** (available if your Apple Watch has watchOS 6 installed). If your Apple Watch has watchOS 3, 4, or 5 installed, select **Allow your Apple Watch to unlock your Mac**. (You can't approve app requests.)

Skip the sign-in and unlock your MacBook Pro

Walk up to your sleeping MacBook Pro wearing your authenticated Apple Watch on your wrist, and lift the cover or press a key to wake your MacBook Pro—Apple Watch unlocks it so you can get right to work.

Approve with Apple Watch

If you're prompted for a password, double-click the side button on your Apple Watch to authenticate your password on your MacBook Pro. You can view your passwords in Safari, approve app installations, unlock a locked note, and more (requires watchOS 6).

How to use AirDrop on your Mac to send files to devices near you

AirDrop lets you wirelessly send documents, photos, map locations, webpages, and more to a nearby Mac, iPhone, or iPad.

Follow these steps to send items using AirDrop.

With AirDrop on your MacBook Pro, you can send items from the Finder, the desktop, or from within apps such as Safari or Maps.

- **From the desktop or a Finder window**: Control-click the item you want to send, choose **Share** and select **AirDrop** from the shortcut menu, then select the device you want to send the item to.
- **From the Finder**: Click **AirDrop** in the Finder sidebar, then drag the item to the device you want to send it to.

- **From an app**: Click the **Share button** in the app's toolbar, choose **AirDrop**, and select the device you want to send the item to.

To receive items using AirDrop, follow these steps.

When someone uses AirDrop to send an item to you on your Mac, you can choose whether to accept and save it. If you send an item from one device to another (for example, from your iPhone to your Mac), and you're signed in to iCloud using the same Apple ID on both devices, the item is automatically accepted and saved.

1. In the AirDrop notification on your MacBook Pro, click the **Accept** pop-up menu, then choose an option.
2. Look for the item in your Downloads folder or the app you saved the item to.

If someone who wants to send you a file can't see your Mac, make sure you've set it up to allow others to send items to you using AirDrop.

To set up AirDrop to allow others to send items to your Mac

1. On your MacBook Pro, click the **Finder icon**   in the Dock to open a Finder window.

2. In the Finder sidebar, click **AirDrop**.

3. In the AirDrop window, click the **Allow me to be discovered by** pop-up menu, then choose an option.

How to use AirPlay to stream what's on your MacBook Pro to an HDMI display or HDTV

AirPlay Mirroring lets you send what's on your MacBook Pro to an HDMI display or HDTV wirelessly with Apple TV. To mirror the MacBook Pro screen on your TV screen or to use the HDTV as a second display, connect your HDTV to Apple TV and make sure the Apple TV is on the same Wi-Fi network as your MacBook Pro.

1. Connect your Mac to the same Wi-Fi network as your Apple TV.

2. On your MacBook Pro, open the app or website that you want to stream video from.

3. In the video playback controls, click the **AirPlay status** icon .
   If you don't see **AirPlay status** icon , go to **Apple** menu, select **System Preferences** and click **Displays**, then select **Show mirroring options in the menu bar when available**.

4. Select your Apple TV.

To stop streaming video, click ⬜ in the video playback controls, then choose **Turn Off AirPlay**.

How to use your iPad as a second display for your Mac (SIDECAR)

With Sidecar, you can use your iPad in landscape orientation as a second display for your MacBook Pro. Like any second display, you can extend your desktop by showing different apps or windows on your iPad, or instead make it show the same ones you see on your MacBook Pro.

1. If you're not already connected to your iPad, click the **Airplay status** icon ⬜ in the menu bar on your MacBook Pro, then select your iPad.
   The **Sidecar** menu ⬜ appears in the menu bar. You can easily change how you work with iPad from the Sidecar menu at any time. For example, switch between using iPad as a mirrored or separate display, or show or hide the sidebar or Touch Bar on iPad.
2. Do any of the following:
   • **Move windows from MacBook Pro to iPad**: Drag a window to the edge of the screen until the pointer appears on your iPad. Or while using an

app, choose **Window** and click **Move Window to iPad**.

- **Move windows from iPad to MacBook Pro**: Drag a window to the edge of the screen until the pointer appears on your MacBook Pro. Or while using an app, choose **Window** and click **Move Window Back to Mac**.

- **Use the sidebar on iPad**: With your finger or Apple Pencil, tap icons in the sidebar to show or hide the menu bar ⬆️, the Dock ⬇️, or the keyboard ⌨️.

- **Switch between the Mac desktop and the iPad on iPad**: Swipe up from the bottom edge of your iPad with one finger to show the iPad Home screen. To show the iPad Dock, swipe up and pause. To show the iPad App Switcher, swipe up and pause in the center of the screen. To return to the Mac desktop, swipe up, then tap the **Sidecar** icon ▪️.

3. When you're ready to stop using your iPad, click the Disconnect icon ◲ at the bottom of the sidebar on iPad. You can also disconnect from the Sidecar menu in the menu bar or in Sidecar or Displays system preferences.

How to insert photos and scans with Continuity Camera on MacBook Pro

With Continuity Camera, you can take a picture or scan a form or document using your nearby iPhone or iPad and have the photo or scan appear instantly on your MacBook Pro, exactly where you need it—for example, in an email, a message, a document, a note, or a folder.

To use Continuity features, follow these steps.

1. On your MacBook Pro, position the cursor where you want to insert a photo or scan.
   For example, in a document, a note, an email, or a text.
2. Choose **File** and select **Import from iPhone or iPad**.
3. Choose **Take Photo** or **Scan Documents**.
4. On your iPhone or iPad, do one of the following:
   - **For a photo**: Take the photo, then tap **Use Photo** or **Retake**.
   - **For a scan**: Take the scan. Your device detects the edges of the document and autocorrects any skewing of the image—if you want to adjust the area included in the scan, drag the frame or its edges. When you're ready, tap **Keep Scan** or **Retake**. When you have the scan you want, tap **Save**.

5. On your MacBook Pro, the picture or scan appears where you positioned the cursor.

  Depending on where the photo or scan is inserted, you can mark it up or adjust other aspects, such as crop it or apply a filter.

How to combine files into a PDF on MacBook Pro

You can quickly combine multiple files into a PDF right from your desktop or a Finder window.

1. On your Mac, click the **Finder icon** in the Dock to open a Finder window.
2. Select the files you want to combine into a PDF.
  Note: The files appear in the PDF in the same order that you select them.
3. Control-click the selected files, then choose **Quick Actions** and click **Create PDF**.
  Alternatively, you can also select the files in the Finder and use the **Create PDF button** in the Preview pane of a Finder window.
  (If you don't see the Preview pane on the right, choose **View** and click **Show Preview**).
4. The file is created automatically with a name similar to the first file you selected.

How to print wirelessly from your MacBook Pro to an AirPrint printer

If you have an AirPrint-enabled printer, you can print photos and documents from your MacBook Pro without having to download and install printer drivers. AirPrint is built into most popular printer models.

To wirelessly print to an AirPrint printer, follow these steps.

1. Make sure your printer is connected to the same Wi-Fi network as your Mac.
2. With a document open on your Mac, choose **File** and select **Print** in the app you're using.
3. Click the **Printer** menu, then choose the **AirPrint printer** under **Nearby Printers**.
4. Select the other print options you want and click **Print**.

How to Connect your AirPods directly with your MacBook Pro

If your AirPods are not connected with your iPhone, you can connect them directly with your MacBook Pro. Follow these steps to connect them directly without first connecting with your iPhone.

1. With your AirPods in their case, open the lid.
2. Press and hold the setup button on the back of the case until the status light flashes white.
3. On your MacBook Pro, choose **Apple** menu and click **System Preferences**.
4. Click **Bluetooth** and select your AirPods in the **Devices list**, then click **Connect**.

How to protect your MacBook Pro from malware

Your MacBook Pro is designed with many features that help protect your laptop and your personal information from malicious software, or malware. One common way malware is distributed is by embedding it in a harmless-looking app. You can reduce this risk by using software only from reliable sources. The settings in Security & Privacy preferences allow you to specify the sources of software installed on your Mac.

1. On your MacBook Pro, choose **Apple** menu and click **System Preferences**.
2. Click **Security & Privacy**, then click **General**.
3. Click the **lock icon** to unlock it, then enter an administrator name and password.
4. Select the sources from which you'll allow software to be installed:

- **App Store**: Allows apps only from the Mac App Store. This is the most secure setting. All the developers of apps in the Mac App Store are identified by Apple, and each app is reviewed before it's accepted. If there's ever a problem with an app, Apple removes it from the Mac App Store.

- **App Store and identified developers**: Allows apps from the Mac App Store and apps from identified developers. Identified developers are registered with Apple and can optionally upload their apps to Apple for a security check. If problems occur with an app, Apple can revoke its authorization.

KEYBOARD SHORTCUTS ON YOUR MACBOOK PRO

You can press key combinations to do things on your MacBook Pro that you'd normally do with a trackpad, mouse, or other device. Here's a list of commonly used keyboard shortcuts.

Shortcut	Description
Command-X	Cut the selected item and copy it to the Clipboard.
Command-C	Copy the selected item to the Clipboard.
Command-V	Paste the contents of the Clipboard into the current document or app.
Command-Z	Undo the previous command. Press Command-Shift-Z to redo.
Command-A	Select all items.
Command-F	Open a Find window, or find items in a document.
Command-G	Find the next occurrence of the item you're searching for. Press Command-Shift-G to find the

previous occurrence.

Command-H	Hide the windows of the front app. Press Command-Option-H to view the front app but hide all other apps.
Command-M	Minimize the front window to the Dock. Press Command-Option-M to minimize all windows of the front app.
Command-N	Open a new document or window.
Command-O	Open the selected item, or open a dialog to select a file to open.
Command-P	Print the current document.
Command-S	Save the current document.
Command-W	Close the front window. Press Command-Option-W to close all windows of the app.
Command-Q	Quit the current app.
Command-Option-Esc	Choose an app to Force Quit.

Command-Tab	Switch to the next most recently used app among your open apps.
Command-Shift-5	Open the Screenshot utility. You can also take screenshots using the following shortcuts:

www.ingramcontent.com/pod-product-compliance
Lightning Source LLC
LaVergne TN
LVHW051747050326
832903LV00029B/2764